W9-ASB-846

CONTENTS

E C L A S S I C S

Great American
Short Stories II

❧

Ambrose
BIERCE

Stories retold by Prescott Hill
Illustrated by James McConnell

LAKE EDUCATION
Belmont, California

LAKE CLASSICS

Great American Short Stories I

Washington Irving, Nathaniel Hawthorne, Mark Twain, Bret Harte, Edgar Allan Poe, Kate Chopin, Willa Cather, Sarah Orne Jewett, Sherwood Anderson, Charles W. Chesnutt

Great American Short Stories II

Herman Melville, Stephen Crane, Ambrose Bierce, Jack London, Edith Wharton, Charlotte Perkins Gilman, Frank R. Stockton, Hamlin Garland, O. Henry, Richard Harding Davis

Great British and Irish Short Stories

Arthur Conan Doyle, Saki (H. H. Munro), Rudyard Kipling, Katherine Mansfield, Thomas Hardy, E. M. Forster, Robert Louis Stevenson, H. G. Wells, John Galsworthy, James Joyce

Great Short Stories from Around the World

Guy de Maupassant, Anton Chekhov, Leo Tolstoy, Selma Lagerlöf, Alphonse Daudet, Mori Ogwai, Leopoldo Alas, Rabindranath Tagore, Fyodor Dostoevsky, Honoré de Balzac

Cover and Text Designer: Diann Abbott

Library of Congress Catalog Number: 94-075024
ISBN 1-56103-016-3
Printed in the United States of America
1 9 8 7 6 5 4 3 2 1

❦ Lake Classic Short Stories ❦

"The universe is made of stories, not atoms."
—Muriel Rukeyser

"The story's about you."
—Horace

Everyone loves a good story. It is hard to think of a friendlier introduction to classic literature. For one thing, short stories are *short*—quick to get into and easy to finish. Of all the literary forms, the short story is the least intimidating and the most approachable.

Great literature is an important part of our human heritage. In the belief that this heritage belongs to everyone, *Lake Classic Short Stories* are adapted for today's readers. Lengthy sentences and paragraphs are shortened. Archaic words are replaced. Modern punctuation and spellings are used. Many of the longer stories are abridged. In all the stories, painstaking care has been taken to preserve the author's unique voice.

Lake Classic Short Stories have something for everyone. The hundreds of stories in the collection cover a broad terrain of themes, story types, and styles. Literary merit was a deciding factor in story selection. But no story was included unless it was as enjoyable as it was instructive. And special priority was given to stories that shine light on the human condition.

Each book in the *Lake Classic Short Stories* is devoted to the work of a single author. Little-known stories of merit are included with famous old favorites. Taken as a whole, the collected authors and stories make up a rich and diverse sampler of the story-teller's art.

Lake Classic Short Stories guarantee a great reading experience. Readers who look for common interests, concerns, and experiences are sure to find them. Readers who bring their own gifts of perception and appreciation to the stories will be doubly rewarded.

❦ Ambrose Bierce ❧
(1842–1914)

About the Author

The mystery surrounding Ambrose Bierce's death is still not solved. At the age of 71, he left San Francisco to join Pancho Villa's rebel army in Mexico. He sent a few letters home describing his experiences. But after those letters, he was never heard from again. One rumor had it that he was killed by a firing squad. Another said that he died of the asthma that had plagued him all his life.

At the age of 24, Bierce arrived in San Francisco aboard a Sacramento riverboat. A native of Indiana, Bierce was six feet tall and had curly blond hair, piercing blue eyes, and a big bushy mustache. In San Francisco he got a job as a night watchman. It was then that he started writing in his spare time.

Bierce's newspaper articles soon made him famous. Readers loved the way he made fun of everyone—especially the powerful. For that he was called the "Wickedest Man in San Francisco" and "Bitter Bierce." From 1886 to 1908, Bierce wrote a column for the San Francisco *Examiner.* In his columns, he even criticized the man who had hired him.

His best-known work is *The Devil's Dictionary.* Here is one of his comic definitions: "Saint, n. A dead sinner, revised and edited."

Bierce's most popular short stories were ghost stories. To get in the mood while he wrote, he kept a skull on his desk. He said that it had belonged to a former friend.

Bierce fought in the Civil War and later wrote about it. *An Occurrence at Owl Creek Bridge* is the most famous of these stories.

If you're a fan of clever writing and ironic humor, Ambrose Bierce is sure to hold your interest.

An Occurrence at Owl Creek Bridge

More than a million men—
in a nation of 35 million—
were killed or wounded in
America's Civil War. This is
a memorable story of one
civilian who was caught in
the clash between the
states.

HIS EYES HAD A KINDLY LOOK—A LOOK THAT SEEMED OUT OF PLACE FOR SOMEONE WITH A ROPE AROUND HIS NECK.

An Occurrence at Owl Creek Bridge

I

A man stood on a railroad bridge in northern Alabama. He looked down into the swift waters 20 feet below him. The man's hands were tied behind his back, and another rope loosely circled his neck. It was tied to a strong wood beam above his head. The slack fell to the level of his knees.

The man stood on one end of a long plank. Two soldiers of the Federal army stood on the other end, holding the plank in place. If they stepped off their end, the plank would tip and the man would drop.

Standing nearby were a sergeant and a captain of the Federal army. The captain had a pistol in his belt. The sergeant was not armed. Even without a weapon, he looked like he might have been a deputy sheriff in civilian life.

At each end of the bridge stood a soldier with a rifle. As sentinels, these men stood tall and straight. Their eyes looked neither right nor left. It was not their duty to know what was happening on the bridge. They were there only to block the foot path that crossed the bridge.

Beyond one of the sentinels, nobody was in sight. The railroad tracks ran straight into a forest for 100 yards. Then they curved and were lost to view. Half a mile farther down the tracks was a small Federal outpost.

Beyond the second sentinel, the stream bank led to open ground with a slight rise. At the top of the rise stood a fort made of tree trunks. Small holes had been cut out of the wall for rifle fire. A bigger hole had also been cut for a cannon. On the slope between the bridge and the fort stood the watchers. They were soldiers from the fort, standing in line at "parade rest." The butts of their rifles were on the ground, the barrels tipped back against their shoulders.

A lieutenant stood at the right of the line, resting his hands on the handle of his sword. He and his men faced the bridge silently. No one moved an inch. The two sentinels on the ends of the bridge stood as still as statues.

The captain at the center of the bridge stood with his arms folded. He didn't move or speak. In silence he watched the sergeant adjust the rope around the man's neck. Death is treated with respect, even by those who know it best. In the code of the army, silence and stillness are ways to show respect.

The man who was about to be hanged looked about 35 years old. He was a civilian, judging by the clothes he wore. He looked like a planter. A nice-looking man, his nose was straight and his mouth firm. His long, dark hair was combed straight back. It touched the collar of his well-fitting coat. He wore a mustache and a pointed beard. His eyes were large and dark gray. They had a kindly look to them—a look that seemed out of place for someone with a rope around his neck.

He didn't look like a common killer. But that didn't mean anything in wartime. Army rules allow the hanging of many kinds of people, even gentlemen.

When everything was ready, the sergeant stepped on the end of the plank where the two soldiers stood. Then the two soldiers stepped away. Now, only the sergeant's weight kept the plank from tipping.

When the captain gave the signal, the sergeant would step off the plank. The plank would tip, and the civilian would drop.

The civilian had to admit it was a simple and effective plan. His eyes had not been covered with a cloth. He looked down at the plank and then at the rushing water below. He saw a piece of wood floating by. His eyes followed it down the current. How slowly it seemed to move! Now the river seemed not to be rushing, but barely moving.

The man closed his eyes. He wanted to fix his last thoughts upon his wife and children. He did not want to think about anything else. But then he heard a sound that took his mind off his dear ones.

It was a sharp sound—like a hammer on steel. He wondered what it was. He could not get it out of his head, but he could not understand what caused it. Was it near to him or far away?

Somehow, it seemed to be both. The sound was steady and slow, like a bell calling people to a funeral. It seemed to grow slower and louder as he listened to it. Finally, it grew so loud that it hurt his ears—like the stabbing of a knife. He tried not to cry out.

What he heard was the ticking of his watch.

He opened his eyes and again saw the water below him. Then the man began to think. "If only I could free my hands! I might throw off the noose and jump into the water. If I dove straight down, I could get away from the bullets. I could swim hard and get to the bank of the stream. Then I could head for the woods and make my way home. Thank God, my home is outside the Federal army's lines! My wife and little ones are still safe."

But as those thoughts ran through the civilian's head, the captain nodded to the sergeant. The sergeant stepped off the plank.

II

Peyton Farquhar was a well-to-do planter of an old, highly respected Alabama family. He was also a slave holder. Like other slave holders, he strongly supported the South in its war against the North. He was not a soldier, but he did whatever he could to help the army of the South. He was not afraid of danger and was willing to do any job he was asked to do. He believed in the old saying that "all is fair in love and war."

One day Farquhar and his wife were sitting on a bench outside their house. A soldier on horseback had ridden up and stopped in front of them. He was wearing the gray uniform of the South. When he asked for a drink of water, Mrs. Farquhar was happy to serve him. While she went to get the water, her husband spoke with the soldier. He asked him if he had any news about the war.

"The Federal soldiers are fixing the railroads," said the soldier. "We heard they've reached Owl Creek Bridge and are coming this way. They've built a fort on one side of the river. The officer in charge there has given an order to his men. He says that any civilian who tries to stop the trains or harm the bridge will be hanged without a trial. I saw the order."

"How far is it to Owl Creek Bridge?" Farquhar asked.

"About 30 miles," said the soldier.

"Are there any Federal soldiers on this side of the creek?" Farquhar asked.

"Just a single guard at this end of the bridge," the soldier answered. "And there's a small outpost next to the railway. That's about half a mile from the bridge."

Farquhar smiled. "Suppose a man—a civilian—should get the better of the guard," he said. "What good could he do?"

The soldier thought for a moment. "I was there a month ago," he said. "I saw that a winter flood had carried a lot of driftwood with it. Some of that driftwood is stuck under the bridge. Now that wood is dry—it would burn very fast."

Mrs. Farquhar came back with the water, which the soldier drank. He thanked her and said good-by to both of them. Then he turned and rode south. That night he passed the plantation again—on his way north. He did not belong to the army of the South as the Farquhars had thought. He was a Federal scout.

III

Peyton Farquhar fell straight down from the bridge, just like a dead man. But then he suddenly awoke from this state—ages later, it seemed to him. What woke him was the sharp pain he felt in his throat. Then the pain spread. It seemed to shoot from his neck all the way down his body. He could not think—he could only feel. Besides the awful pain, he felt as though he were moving. First he could feel himself dropping through the air, and then suddenly his feet hit something. He felt his feet go through it. He felt cold. He felt wet.

But now he could think again! He knew that the rope had broken and that he had fallen into the stream. He wasn't swallowing water, for the noose was still tight around his throat. It kept the water from going to his lungs. Then a strange thought came to him—could he die of hanging at the bottom of a river? The idea seemed mad.

Farquhar opened his eyes in the blackness and saw light above him. For a moment or two he knew he was sinking. The light grew fainter until it was almost gone. But then it started to get brighter, and he knew he was rising toward the surface.

"To be hanged and drowned," he thought, "is not so bad. But I do not wish to be shot. No, I will not be shot. That is not fair."

He felt a pain in his wrists as he tried to free his hands. He twisted and pulled as he floated upward. Finally his hands were free. Quickly he reached for the noose and took it from around his neck. He pushed it away from him, as if it were a snake.

Then he thought, "Put it back! Put it back!" as he felt a new stab of pain. He was starving for air and his brain seemed on fire. His heart seemed about to leap out of his mouth—but his hands would not obey his brain. They would not reach for the noose. Instead, they beat the water with quick downward strokes. The movements forced his body to the surface of the stream.

Suddenly his head came out of the water. His eyes were blinded by the sunlight. He took in a huge breath of air, then he let it out with a scream.

Now he was fully awake and in control of his body. He turned toward the forest on the bank of the stream. Everything looked so clear. He seemed to see each tree by itself. He could even see the leaves and the veins in the leaves. He noticed the insects, too, and the bright green flies. He noticed the gray spiders and their webs that stretched from twig to twig.

Now he could hear more clearly than he ever had heard before. He heard the hum of bees in the flowers and the beating of a dragonfly's wings. When a fish swam by, he seemed to hear the rush of its body as it parted the water.

Farquhar had come to the surface, facing downstream. Now he turned in the water and saw the bridge, the fort, and the soldiers. He saw the captain, the sergeant, and the two privates—the men who had tried to hang him. They shouted and waved their arms at him. The captain had drawn his pistol, but had not fired. The sergeant and the two privates didn't have guns.

Suddenly he heard a sharp sound. Something hit the water a few inches from his head, splashing water in his face. Then he heard a second sharp sound, just like the first. He looked toward one end of the bridge and saw a sentinel with his rifle at his shoulder. A cloud of blue smoke rose from its barrel. He could see the sentinel's eye looking down at him. It was a gray eye. For some reason he remembered having heard that gray eyes were the keenest. All the best shots were said to have gray eyes. But this shot had missed.

He turned again and looked at the forest on the stream bank. Then he heard a loud high voice behind him. It was louder than any other sound. Farquhar was no soldier, but he knew what that sound meant. It was the order of the lieutenant on shore. The cruel words rang out, "Attention company.... Shoulder arms.... Ready.... Aim.... Fire!"

Farquhar dived—dived as deeply as he could. The water roared in his ears like a waterfall, yet he still heard the thunder of the rifles. He saw the shining bits of metal come through the water. Most lost speed and fell to the bottom of the stream. But one hot bit of metal got caught between his collar and his neck. He pulled it out and let it fall.

Then Farquhar rose to the surface again, gasping for air. He realized he had been under for a long time. Now he was much farther downstream—nearer to safety. The soldiers had just about finished reloading their rifles. The two sentinels on the bridge fired again, but missed him.

The hunted man watched them over his shoulder. Now he was swimming with the current as fast as he could. His brain was as active as his arms and legs. His thoughts were coming as fast as lightning bolts.

"The officer won't make that mistake again," he thought. "When they all fire at once, it's as easy to dive as when just one man fires. Now he'll let them fire whenever they want to. God help me, I can't get away from them all."

Just then there was a huge splash in front of him and a loud bang from the fort. A rising sheet of water curved over him. It fell on him, blinded him, choked him. They had fired the cannon at him!

Suddenly he felt himself spinning around like a top. The water, the forest, the bridge, the fort, and the soldiers were all a blur. He could not make out forms, but only colors. Streaks and circles of color flashed by his eyes. As if he were caught in a whirlpool, he was spinning so fast that it made him sick to his stomach.

A few minutes later he washed up on the south bank. He had gone around a bend of the stream, out of sight of the bridge and the fort. Here he was hidden from his enemies.

Farquhar wept with delight. He shouted his thanks aloud. He dug his fingers into the sand, and threw it in the air. To him it looked like gold, like diamonds, rubies, emeralds. He could think of nothing beautiful that the sand did not look like.

Everything looked beautiful! The trees on the stream bank looked like giant garden plants. They seemed to be lined up in perfect order. All of their blossoms seemed to have a beautiful smell. A strange, rosy light shone through the spaces between their trunks. The wind in the leaves sounded like harp music. Now he had no wish to finish his escape. He was happy to stay in this magic spot.

Just then the sound of bullets in the branches overhead woke him from his dream. He jumped to his feet and rushed deeper into the forest.

All that day he kept moving. He used the sun to guide him toward home. But the forest seemed to never end—there was no break in it, not even a hunter's road. Before, he had never realized that he lived in such a wild part of the world.

By nightfall he was worn out. His feet hurt, and he was very hungry. Only the thought of his wife and children kept him going. At last he found a road that he knew would take him home. It was as wide and straight as a city street, but it was empty. There were no fields next to it. There were no houses anywhere. There was no hint that people lived nearby—not even a barking dog.

The black bodies of the great trees formed a straight wall on both sides of the road. Great golden stars were shining in the sky above. For some reason they looked strange to him. They seemed to be in groups that he had never seen before. Sadly, they seemed like unlucky stars to him.

As he walked, he could hear strange noises coming from the forest. Once or twice he thought he heard whispers. But they were in an unknown language.

His neck was in terrible pain. When he lifted his hands to it, he found it was horribly swollen. He knew there was a circle of black where the rope had choked him. His eyes were hot and puffy. He could no longer close them. And his tongue was swollen with thirst. His only relief was in opening his mouth wide and taking in the cool air.

Now his path seemed covered with a soft layer of grass. He could no longer feel the road beneath his feet. Where was he? He must have fallen asleep while he was walking. For now he sees another scene. He is standing at the gate of his own home. All is as he had left it—bright and beautiful in the morning sunshine. He must have walked the entire night.

He pushes open the gate and walks up the wide, white path. His wife looks fresh and cool as she rushes down the porch steps to meet him. Now she stands at the bottom of the steps, a smile of great joy on her face. Ah, how beautiful she is!

He springs forward with open arms. As he is about to hug her, he feels a blow on the back of his neck. A blinding white light blazes all about him. He hears a sound like the roar of a cannon. Then all is darkness and silence.

Peyton Farquhar was dead. His neck was broken. His body swung gently from side to side beneath the Owl Creek Bridge.

A Horseman
in the Sky

The American Civil War
tore apart not only the
country, but often families
as well. In this chilling
story, a sleeping sentinel
has a rude awakening. How
can he know where his duty
lies?

THE SENTINEL'S DUTY WAS CLEAR. THE MAN MUST BE
SHOT DEAD WITHOUT WARNING.

A Horseman
in the Sky

I

It was a sunny afternoon in the autumn of the year 1861. A soldier was lying near a road in western Virginia. Hidden by a clump of trees, he was stretched out full length on his stomach. His feet were resting on his toes, and his head was on his left arm. In his right hand, he loosely held his rifle.

Except for a small movement of his body, he seemed to be dead. He was not dead, though. He was a sentinel, and he was asleep at his post of duty. If someone caught him, he would soon be dead. That was the just and legal penalty for sleeping on duty.

The clump of trees in which he lay was at the top of a hill. On his right, the road dropped sharply down to the south. To his left was an even higher hill. On that hilltop was a flat rock that stuck out to the north. The rock capped a high cliff that overlooked a deep valley. A stone dropped from the rock would fall straight down for more than 1,000 feet.

The young soldier lay on another part of that same cliff. If he had been awake, he could have seen both the road and the rock. He could also have seen the steep cliff below the rock and all the valley. It might have made him dizzy to see such a sight.

The country all around him was mostly covered with woods. In the valley, though, there was a small green meadow with a little stream flowing through it.

It could barely be seen from the cliff. In fact, the meadow didn't look much bigger than an ordinary back yard. But it really covered several acres. Its green color was much brighter than that of the woods around it. On the other side of the valley rose another giant cliff. It looked much like the cliff on which the soldier was sleeping.

The valley seemed to be cut off from all sides. It was hard to believe that a stream ran through it. It was even harder to believe that a road ran through it and up both cliffs. The valley seemed wild and untouched by humans. But that was not the case.

No country is so wild and hard to reach that men will not fight wars there. Hidden in the woods below were about 4,000 soldiers of the Federal army. In the current war, that was the army of the North. The sleeping soldier was a member of that army.

The men had marched all day and night. Now they were resting in a place out of sight. Only when it got dark would they take to the road once again. They could not afford to be seen by the enemy. Because there was only one road into it and one road out, the valley was like a trap.

When nightfall came, all 4,000 soldiers would climb to the hilltop where the young man was sleeping. Then about midnight they would go down the other side of the hill. That was where the enemy soldiers of the South were camped. The Federal soldiers hoped to surprise them by sneaking around behind them. If they could do that, they were sure to win a victory.

But if they failed, they would be in very deep trouble. And they *would* fail if the enemy found out they were camped in the valley.

II

The sleeping soldier in the clump of trees was a young Virginian named Carter Druse. He was the son of wealthy parents, an only child. Growing up in the mountains of western Virginia, he had enjoyed an easy life. His home was only a few miles from where he now lay. One morning he got up from the breakfast table and made an announcement. "Father," he said, "Federal soldiers have arrived at Grafton. I am going to join their army."

The father lifted his head and looked at his son in silence. Then he said, "Well, go, sir. And whatever happens, do what you think is your duty. The state of Virginia—to which you are a traitor—must get along without you. Should we both live to the end of the war, we will talk more about this. The doctor has told you that your mother is very ill. She cannot live much longer than another two weeks. It would be best not to tell her what you are about to do. It would upset her too much."

So, Carter Druse bowed to his father and said good-by. His father returned the bow, even though he thought his heart would break. Then the young man left his childhood home to become a soldier.

A brave young man, Carter Druse made many friends among his fellow soldiers. Because of his bravery and because he knew the countryside, he was chosen for sentinel duty. It was an important job, and he seemed the best man to do it.

Still, his bravery could not overcome his need to sleep. He had been up too long and was very tired. The simple fact was that he had fallen asleep on duty.

Who can say what good or bad angel came in a dream to wake him? But without a movement, without a sound, *something* seemed to touch him. Some spirit seemed to whisper in his ear. For no good reason, he suddenly woke up.

The young soldier quietly raised his head from his arm. His hand closed around his rifle as he looked out from the clump of trees.

He smiled at the sight that greeted him. On the high rock to his left, he saw what he thought was a statue. A man on horseback was outlined against the sky. The man and the horse were so still that they looked like they were carved from stone. The man wore gray—the uniform of the enemy. In one hand he held a rifle. In the other he held the horse's reins.

The lone rider was looking out over the valley. His face was turned away from the sentinel. All the young soldier could make out was part of the man's brow and the shadow of his beard.

But the man's uniform told the sentinel what he most needed to know.

The man belonged to the army of the
South. Outlined against the sky, he and
his horse seemed like giants.

For a moment, Carter Druse had a
strange feeling. He felt as though he
might have slept until the end of the
war. He thought the statue before him
might have been put up in memory of a
fallen soldier. But that feeling left him
quickly. The statue moved slightly. The
horse stepped back a little from the
edge of the cliff, although the rider
himself did not move.

Now, the young sentinel was wide
awake. He realized just what was
happening. He slowly raised his rifle and
brought the butt against his cheek. He
moved the barrel forward and looked
down the sights. He aimed directly at the
rider's chest.

A touch upon the trigger just then—
and all would have been well with Carter
Druse. But at that instant, the rider
turned. He looked in the sentinel's

direction. He seemed to look right into the young man's eyes. That look went directly into Carter's brave, kind heart.

Is it then so terrible to kill an enemy in war? What if the enemy has learned a secret? What if that knowledge can mean an awful loss for your side?

Carter Druse grew pale. He shook all over. Trembling from head to foot, he felt faint. The rider and horse before him now looked blurry. His hands fell away from his rifle, and his head slowly dropped until his face rested on the ground. The brave young soldier was close to passing out.

The feeling passed quickly. In another moment, he raised his face from the ground. Again he clamped his hands on his rifle. His mind and his heart were clear now, and he knew what he had to do. His finger moved toward the trigger.

He could not hope to capture the enemy. If he tried, the man would ride off to his camp and sound the alarm. The sentinel's duty was clear. The man must be shot dead without warning.

But no—there was still a hope. *Maybe the rider had seen nothing.* Maybe he was just enjoying the view. If that was so, the sentinel could allow him to ride away. Carter Druse decided that he could tell by the way the man rode. If he was not in a hurry, that meant he had seen nothing.

Then the young man looked down to the valley. There in the meadow he could see a long line of men and horses. Some foolish officer was allowing the men to water the horses in plain view!

Druse looked away from the valley and back toward the cliff. He raised his rifle and aimed it. This time he pointed it at the horse. In his head he seemed to hear his father's words, "Whatever happens, do what you think is your duty."

He was calm now. His nerves were as relaxed as a sleeping baby's. His breathing was slow and steady. Then he held his breath as he took aim. His sense of duty had won. He fired.

III

An officer of the Federal army had left the camp in the valley. The Federal troops would not be starting out until dark. Until then, the officer had decided to do some scouting. He walked toward a cliff on one side of the valley. When he was about a quarter of a mile from the cliff, he stopped and looked up. High above the tops of the pine trees, he could see a huge rock. Jutting out from the cliff, the rock was outlined against the sky.

As the officer looked upward, he saw a strange sight. A man on horseback seemed to come riding down through the air.

The rider sat straight up, like a soldier, holding onto the reins with one hand. His long hair streamed back from his bare head. The horse's mane was streaming back like the man's hair. The animal's body was level. Its legs moved as though it were running on the ground. But this was a wild flight through the air!

The sight of the horseman in the sky filled the officer with wonder and terror. His legs gave way under him, and he fell to the ground. At the same time he heard a crashing sound in the trees. Then the sound died without an echo—and all was still.

The officer got to his feet, shaking. His shin was sore from the fall he had taken. The pain brought him back to his senses. Pulling himself together, he ran for a point some distance from the foot of the cliff. He expected to find the man and the horse there. He didn't.

It had only taken a short time for the horse and rider to fall. Surprised as he was, the officer had not been thinking clearly. It seemed to him that the horse had been moving forward—as though on a march. The horse had seemed to move through the air with such ease that the officer had been fooled. In fact, the horse and rider had fallen straight down. The officer should have looked right at the foot of the cliff. A half hour later he returned to camp.

This officer was a wise man. He knew better than to tell a true story that no one would believe. He said nothing of what he had seen.

IV

After firing his shot, Carter Druse reloaded his rifle and continued watching. About ten minutes later, a Federal sergeant came crawling toward him on hands and knees. Druse did not turn his head nor look at him. He just stayed the way he was.

"Did you fire?" the sergeant asked.

"Yes," the young man answered.

"At what?" said the sergeant.

"A horse," Druse said. "It was standing on that big rock, pretty far out. You see that it is no longer there. It went over the cliff."

The sentinel's face was white, but there was no other sign of his feelings. Having answered, he turned away and said no more. The sergeant did not understand.

"See here, Druse," the sergeant said, "it's no use making a mystery. I order you to report. Was there anybody on the horse?"

"Yes," the young man said.

"Well, who was it?" asked the sergeant.

"My father."

The sergeant got to his feet and walked away. "Good God!" he said.

❧

The Applicant

Do good people usually get what they deserve? If so, old Amasa Abersush has certainly earned his reward. Look for the ironic twist in this story of a generous man in search of generosity.

"THE TRUSTEES HAVE DECIDED THAT YOUR APPLICATION
DISAGREES WITH THEM."

The Applicant

A small sturdy boy waded through the deep snow that had fallen overnight. His little sister followed him, laughing with glee. They were the children of one of Grayville's best-known citizens, Deacon Byram. As the boy moved forward, his foot struck something that was buried in the snow. There was no way to tell what the thing was, because it was completely covered. It is the purpose of this story to explain how it came to be there.

Anyone who has visited Grayville has seen the big stone building on the hill. It is north of the railway station—on the right side of the road to Great Mowbray.

The building is dull looking. It appears to have been built by someone who didn't want it to be looked at too closely. Because it was on top of a hill, it could not be hidden. But the builder did what he could to keep people from taking a second look.

To be sure, the Abersush Home for Old Men does not invite human attention. But dull-looking as it is, it is a very large building. It cost a great deal of money to build.

Amasa Abersush, the man who paid for the building, enjoyed giving money to charity. He was a true *philanthropist*. As a young man in Boston, he had owned many ships. Then he had doubled his fortune by buying and selling tea, silk, and spices from Asia.

The building had cost a lot. But Amasa Abersush had given even more money than that. He also gave money to take care of the building and the people who would live there. It came to more than half a million dollars.

After the Home was built, Amasa Abersush left the town of Grayville. He went off across the sea in one of his ships. No one knew why. Some said it was because he could not stand the sight of the building. Others said that he went off to find a wife.

One man joked that the "bachelor philanthropist" left town because so many women wanted to marry him.

Whatever the case, he had not returned to Grayville in many years. But the people of that town had heard rumors of his travels. No one knew for sure if the stories were true. The younger people of the town had never seen the man. To them, he was no more than a name. But from above the door of the Abersush Home for Old Men, that name shouted out in stone.

No matter how it looks from the outside, the Home serves its purpose. It offers a place for the poor, old men who live there. Without the Home, they might die in the streets. At the time I speak of, there were about 20 men living there.

A man named Silas Tilbody also lived there, along with his family. He was the superintendent. It was his job to manage the place. He often said that it seemed there were at least 100 men living there. That, he said, was because the old men argued and complained so much. Mr. Tilbody did not see what they had to complain about. He felt that the poor, old men should be more thankful for having a free place to live.

Whenever one of the men in the Home died, another poor man was taken in to fill his place. Mr. Tilbody was not happy about that, either. He thought that taking in only poor people would just make his own life harder. He would have liked the Home to be a kind of "castle in Spain." He, of course, would be in charge. If he had his way, the Home would only take in men who could pay. And he did not want old men who complained. He wanted cheerful, younger men who wouldn't cause him any problems.

Also, Mr. Tilbody wanted to be free of the Home's trustees. They were the people who told him what to do. At their meetings, they decided how Amasa Abersush's money should be spent. They watched the money carefully.

The trustees believed that the men who lived in the Home did not deserve much. Weren't they to blame for being poor? The trustees thought that the men should have been more thrifty when they were young. If they had, they would not now be poor. The trustees were very thrifty when it came to spending money. They spent as little as possible on buying food for the Home. And they were stingy with coal for the big furnace.

The trustees also decided who should be allowed to live in the Home. Mr. Tilbody had to follow their orders. But he did not see any need for trustees. He thought he could handle things very well without their help.

The men who lived in the Home did not care what Mr. Tilbody or the trustees thought. They lived out the last years of their lives as best they could. When they went to the grave, they were replaced by other men much like them. This story is about such a man, one who came to the Home on a cold winter night.

The old man did not seem interested in appearances. At least he did not pay much attention to what he himself looked like. Even in winter, his clothes seemed to belong to another time of year—and another place. They looked like something you might see in the summer—on a farm. In short, they looked like they might belong to a scarecrow standing in a field.

As the old man walked up Abersush Street toward the Home, he moved slowly. Someone watching might have thought a scarecrow had come to life. His clothes looked like rags, but they were not out of place. After all, they showed how poor he was. And the Home was a place for poor, old men. Except for the superintendent and his family, of course.

It was snowing as the old man passed through he gates of the Home. The path leading up to the large building was already drifted in white. From time to time the old man stopped to brush the snow from his clothes. He would go on a few steps, then stop again to brush away the snow.

Finally he reached the stairs. He climbed them slowly. At the top of the steps, a large light burned over the main door. He stood under the light for a while, then turned to his left. It seemed as if he did not want to be seen that clearly. So he walked along the face of the building until he came to a smaller door. There he rang the bell and waited.

The door was opened by the great Mr. Tilbody himself. The old man took off his hat and held it in his hand.

Mr. Tilbody did not look surprised to see the man. And he did not look unhappy. In fact, Mr. Tilbody was in a very good mood. His chubby face and pale blue eyes seemed to shine. That had much to do with the time of year. It was Christmas Eve, and he seemed to be filled with holiday spirit.

Mr. Tilbody was wearing his hat, boots, and coat. In his hand he held an umbrella. It seemed clear that he was going out into the snowstorm. In fact, he was on his way to do an act of charity. He had just left his wife and children in their warm living room. Now he was going to go downtown to do some Christmas shopping.

The superintendent did not ask the old man to step inside. But he said, "Hello! You're just in time. If you had come a minute later, you would have missed me. Hurry now—I have no time to waste. We will walk a little way together."

"Thank you," said the old man. His thin, white face had a sad look on it. "But, if the trustees—if my application—"

Mr. Tilbody stepped outside, closing the door behind him. It cut off the light from inside the building. Then he turned to the old man and spoke. His words cut off another kind of light for the old man. They closed another kind of door for him.

Mr. Tilbody told the old man, "The trustees have decided that your application disagrees with them."

Mr. Tilbody smiled. He thought he had put the news in a humorous way.

But the old man did not seem to get the joke. At any rate, he did not laugh.

Instead, he said, "Oh, my God!" His voice was thin and soft. To Mr. Tilbody, it sounded weak. The sadness in the old man's face seemed to have no effect on him.

The old man was looking down at the snow. He seemed to be trying to follow the tracks he had made earlier. Mr. Tilbody was walking slowly to stay near him.

"It is true," Mr. Tilbody said. "The trustees have all agreed that you should not be admitted to the Home. Deacon Byram, who is a trustee, told me why. The fact is—it could be embarrassing to us. In the letter you sent me, you told me about your needs. Surely, you are old enough and poor enough to be admitted to the Home. That is clear to us. But having you here might not look good to the public. After thinking it over, we decided it would be better for the Home if you went somewhere else."

By now they were out on the street. The dim light from a street lamp shone through the falling snowflakes. The tracks of the old man's footsteps had been covered up completely. He did not seem to know which way to go.

Mr. Tilbody had started to walk faster. When he was a short distance away, he turned back to look at the old man.

He started to speak to the old man. "I am sorry, but—" he said. But the old man did not hear. Or if he heard, the words meant nothing to him. He had crossed the street into an empty lot. He did not seem to know where he was going. But since he had nowhere to go, that was not surprising.

Mr. Tilbody shook his head and continued on his way.

And that is how it happened that the son of Deacon Byram made his discovery. The next day was Christmas. The church bells were ringing as the sturdy small

boy and his sister pushed their way
through the snow. It was then that he
struck his foot against something that
was buried beneath the snow. It was the
body of Amasa Abersush, philanthropist.

The Imperfect Conflagration

How can a big fire be "imperfect"? This tongue-in-cheek story is told from the outrageous viewpoint of a criminal mind. Read on to find out what was wrong with the fire.

IT WAS THAT MUSIC BOX WHICH BROUGHT DISASTER AND
DISGRACE UPON OUR FAMILY.

The Imperfect Conflagration

Early one June morning in 1872, I murdered my father. The act made a deep impression on me at the time. This was before my marriage, while I was living with my parents in Wisconsin. My father and I were in the library of our home. We were dividing up the proceeds from a burglary we had committed that night. These were household things mostly, and dividing them equally was hard work.

We got on very well with the napkins, towels, and such things. The silverware was shared pretty fairly, too. But you can see for yourself the trouble in dividing one music box between two people.

It was that music box which brought disaster and disgrace upon our family. If we had left it alone, my poor father might now be alive.

The music box was a beautiful piece of workmanship. It was inlaid with costly wood and carved with odd designs. And it could do much more than play a great many tunes! It could whistle like a quail and bark like a dog. It also crowed every morning at daybreak—whether or not it had been wound up.

That music box could also break the Ten Commandments. That trick really won my father's heart. It caused him to commit the only truly dishonorable act of his life. (Although he might have committed more if he had lived longer.)

First he tried to hide the music box from me, and then he lied about taking it. But I knew that his main reason for committing the burglary was to get the unusual music box.

My father had the music box hidden under his cloak. Both of us had worn cloaks by way of disguise. He had sworn to me that he did not take it. Of course, I knew that he had. And I knew something else besides that. I knew that the music box would crow at daybreak and betray him. I had to make sure we didn't finish dividing the goods until then.

It all happened just as I knew it would. As the light from outside began to appear, I heard a long cock-a-doodle-do from under my father's cloak. The rooster crow was followed by some notes of music and ended with a click.

We had used a small ax to break into the house. Now it lay between us on the table, and I picked it up. The old man saw that he could no longer hide the music box. He took it from under his coat and set it out on the table.

"Cut it in two, if you prefer that plan," he said. "I was only trying to keep it from being ruined."

He was a lover of music and knew how to play the accordion with much feeling.

"I do not question the purity of your motive," I said. "I do not want to judge my own father—I don't think that would be right. But business is business—and I may have to end our partnership with this ax. It depends on whether you let me search you after all of our future burglaries."

"No," he said, after thinking it over for a while. "I could not allow that. It would look like I wasn't honest. People would say that you didn't trust me."

I could not help admiring his spirit. For a moment I was proud of him and ready to overlook his fault. But a look at the jewels on the music box changed my mind. As I said at the start, I removed him from the world.

Having done so, I felt a little uneasy. Not only was he my own dear father, but his body might be found. It was now broad daylight. I knew that my mother would soon be coming into the library. In fact, that is just what happened. So I thought it best to get rid of her, too— which I did. Then I paid off all our servants and fired them.

That afternoon I went to see the chief of police. I told him what I had done and asked his advice. It would have been painful to me if everyone found out what I had done. Many people would hold it against me. The newspapers would bring it up if I ever ran for office.

The chief agreed with me. He himself had killed a lot of people. After talking with his friend the judge, he advised me to hide the bodies in a bookcase. He said

I should take out a big insurance policy on the house. Then, he said, I should burn the house down. So I set about doing all that.

In the library was a bookcase my father had bought from an inventor. Because of its glass doors, it looked something like a cabinet. I took out the shelves and put my parents inside it. They were now stiff enough so that they stood straight up. I locked the doors and draped some curtains over the outside of the glass. The man I bought the insurance from walked by the case six times without suspecting a thing.

That night, after I got the policy, I set fire to the house. I was two miles away from the house when a neighbor found me. With cries of worry about my dear parents, I rushed to the scene of the blazing fire.

The whole town had shown up there. My parents' house and everything in it had burned down completely, except for the bookcase. It was still standing in the middle of the smoking ashes. The bookcase was unharmed except for the curtains, which had burned away.

Inside stood my parents. Not a hair on either of their heads was burned. Even their clothes were untouched by the fire. Everyone could see the injuries that my ax had done to their heads and throats. But no one said a word. They were all too terrified to speak. I myself was greatly affected by the sight.

Some three years later, I had almost forgotten about it all. I had gone to New York City to help get rid of some counterfeit money. Passing the window of a furniture store, I saw a bookcase just like my father's.

I went into the store and asked where the bookcase had come from. "I bought it cheap from a reformed inventor," the store owner told me. "He said it was fireproof. The wood is supposed to be treated with a special chemical. The glass is supposed to be fireproof, too. Of course, I don't believe that it *really* is fireproof. So I'll sell it to you for the price of an ordinary bookcase."

"No," I said. "If you can't guarantee that it's fireproof, I won't buy it." Then I said good-by and walked out of the store.

I would not have bought it at any price. It brought back memories that were very disagreeable.

Thinking About
the Stories

An Occurrence at Owl Creek Bridge

1. How important is the background of the story? Is weather a factor in the story? Is there a war going on or some other unusual circumstance? What influence does the background have on the characters' lives?

2. Who is the main character in this story? Who are one or two of the minor characters? Describe each of these characters in one or two sentences.

3. Imagine that you have been asked to write a short review of this story. In one or two sentences, tell what the story is about and why someone would enjoy reading it.

A Horseman in the Sky

1. The plot is the series of events that takes place in a story. Usually, story events are linked in some way. Can you name an event in this story that was the cause of a later event?

2. Compare and contrast at least two characters in this story. In what ways are they alike? In what ways are they different?

3. Does the main character in this story have an internal conflict? Does a terrible decision have to be made? Explain the character's choices.

The Applicant

1. Which character in this story do you most admire? Why? Which character do you like the least?

2. Interesting story plots often have unexpected twists and turns. What surprises did you find in this story?

3. Suppose this story had a completely different outcome. Can you think of another effective ending for this story?

An Imperfect Conflagration

1. Look back at the illustration that introduces this story. What character or characters are pictured? What is happening in the scene? What clues does the picture give you about the time and place of the story?

2. An author builds the plot around the conflict in a story. In this story, what forces or characters are struggling against each other? How is the conflict finally resolved?

3. Good writing always has an effect on the reader. How did you feel when you finished reading this story? Were you surprised, horrified, amused, sad, touched, or inspired? What elements in the story made you feel that way?

8